To

_____

From

_____

Occasion

_____

a bouquet of

Beautiful Blessings

 to warm your heart

Tyndale House Publishers, Inc.

CAROL STREAM, ILLINOIS

Be careful to obey all these commands I am
giving you. Show love to the LORD your God
by walking in his ways and holding tightly
to him. . . . Look, today I am giving you the
choice between a blessing and a curse! You
will be blessed if you obey the commands
of the LORD your God that I am giving
you today.

DEUTERONOMY 11:22, 26-27

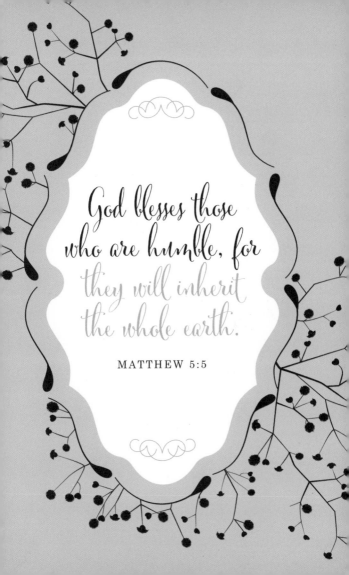

God blesses those
who are humble, for
they will inherit
the whole earth.

MATTHEW 5:5

Don't be
afraid,
little flock.
For it
gives your Father
great happiness
to give you
the Kingdom.

LUKE 12:32

The LORD longs to be gracious to you; therefore he will rise up to show you compassion. For the LORD is a God of justice. Blessed are all who wait for him! . . . Whether you turn to the right or to the left, your ears will hear a voice behind you, saying, "This is the way; walk in it."

ISAIAH 30:18, 21, NIV

God has now revealed to us his mysterious will regarding Christ—which is to fulfill his own good plan. And this is the plan: At the right time he will bring everything together under the authority of Christ—everything in heaven and on earth. Furthermore, because we are united with Christ, we have received an inheritance from God, for he chose us in advance.

EPHESIANS 1:9-11

*Give thanks
to the* LORD,
for he is good!
*His faithful
love endures
forever.*

1 CHRONICLES 16:34

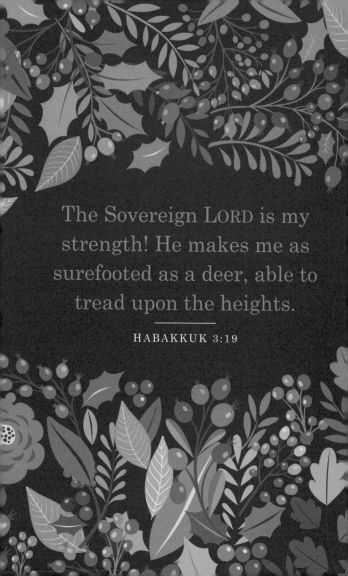

The Sovereign LORD is my strength! He makes me as surefooted as a deer, able to tread upon the heights.

———

HABAKKUK 3:19

As God's grace reaches more and more
people, there will be great thanksgiving,
and God will receive more and more glory.
That is why we never give up. Though our
bodies are dying, our spirits are being
renewed every day. For our present troubles
are small and won't last very long. Yet
they produce for us a glory that vastly
outweighs them and will last forever!

2 CORINTHIANS 4:15-17

What, then, shall we say in response to these things? If God is for us, who can be against us? He who did not spare his own Son, but gave him up for us all—how will he not also, along with him, graciously give us all things? Who will bring any charge against those whom God has chosen? It is God who justifies.

ROMANS 8:31-33, NIV

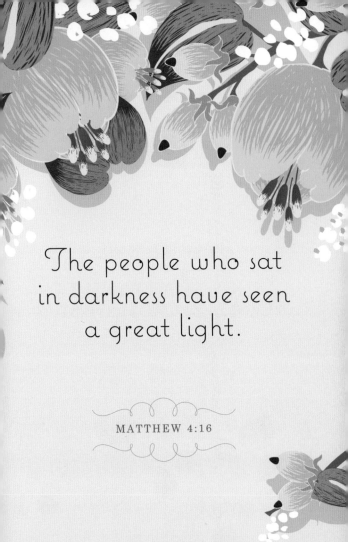

The people who sat
in darkness have seen
a great light.

MATTHEW 4:16

Blessed are you

WHEN PEOPLE INSULT
YOU . . . BECAUSE OF ME.

MATTHEW 5:11, NIV

Rejoice insofar as you share Christ's sufferings, that you may also rejoice and be glad when his glory is revealed. If you are insulted for the name of Christ, you are blessed, because the Spirit of glory and of God rests upon you.

1 PETER 4:13-14, ESV

"Bring all the tithes into the storehouse so there will be enough food in my Temple. If you do," says the LORD of Heaven's Armies, "I will open the windows of heaven for you. I will pour out a blessing so great you won't have enough room to take it in! Try it! Put me to the test! . . . Then all nations will call you blessed."

MALACHI 3:10, 12

Blessed are those
who are generous,
because they
feed the poor.

PROVERBS 22:9

*I will cause
showers to
come down in
their season;
there shall be
showers of
blessing.*

EZEKIEL 34:26, NKJV

God has put all things under the authority
of Christ and has made him head over all
things for the benefit of the church. And
the church is his body; it is made full and
complete by Christ, who fills all things
everywhere with himself.

EPHESIANS 1:22-23

The LORD,
the LORD himself,
is my strength
and my defense;
he has become
my salvation.

ISAIAH 12:2, NIV

Blessed is the one
whose sin
the LORD does not
count against them
and in whose spirit
is no deceit.

PSALM 32:2, NIV

To the faithful you show yourself faithful; to those with integrity you show integrity. To the pure you show yourself pure, but to the crooked you show yourself shrewd. You rescue the humble, but you humiliate the proud. . . . For who is God except the LORD? Who but our God is a solid rock? God arms me with strength, and he makes my way perfect.

PSALM 18:25-27, 31-32

Love is patient and kind. Love is not
jealous or boastful or proud or rude. It
does not demand its own way. It is not
irritable, and it keeps no record of being
wronged. It does not rejoice about injustice
but rejoices whenever the truth wins out.
Love never gives up, never loses faith,
is always hopeful, and endures through
every circumstance.

1 CORINTHIANS 13:4-7

*This is how
God showed his
love among us:*
He sent his
one and only
Son into
the world.

1 JOHN 4:9, NIV

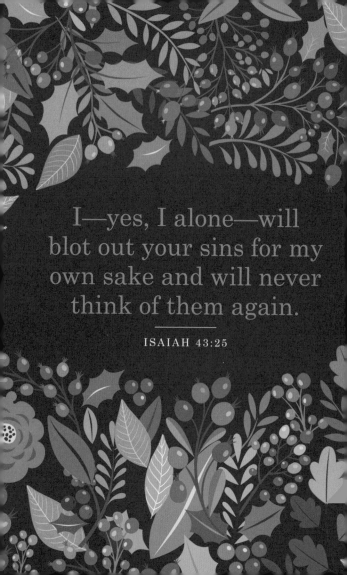

I—yes, I alone—will blot out your sins for my own sake and will never think of them again.

ISAIAH 43:25

This is the message we heard from Jesus
and now declare to you: God is light, and
there is no darkness in him at all. . . .
If we are living in the light, as God is
in the light, then we have fellowship with
each other, and the blood of Jesus, his
Son, cleanses us from all sin.

1 JOHN 1:5, 7

Children, obey your parents because you belong to the Lord, for this is the right thing to do. "Honor your father and mother." This is the first commandment with a promise: If you honor your father and mother, "things will go well for you, and you will have a long life on the earth."

EPHESIANS 6:1-3

Children are
a gift from the
LORD; they are
a reward from him.

PSALM 127:3

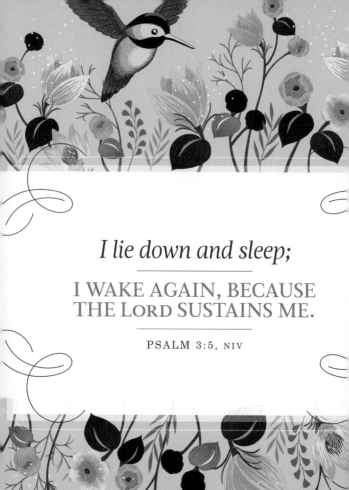

I lie down and sleep;

I WAKE AGAIN, BECAUSE
THE Lord SUSTAINS ME.

PSALM 3:5, NIV

Just as you accepted Christ Jesus as your Lord, you must continue to follow him. Let your roots grow down into him, and let your lives be built on him. Then your faith will grow strong in the truth you were taught, and you will overflow with thankfulness.

COLOSSIANS 2:6-7

If you make the LORD your refuge, if you make the Most High your shelter, no evil will conquer you; no plague will come near your home. For he will order his angels to protect you wherever you go.

PSALM 91:9-11

When I am afraid,
I will put my
trust in you.

PSALM 56:3

Show hospitality to strangers, for some who have done this have entertained angels without realizing it!

HEBREWS 13:2

All praise to God, the Father of our Lord Jesus Christ. God is our merciful Father and the source of all comfort. He comforts us in all our troubles so that we can comfort others. When they are troubled, we will be able to give them the same comfort God has given us.

2 CORINTHIANS 1:3-4

God blesses those who mourn, for they will be comforted.

MATTHEW 5:4

You have every spiritual gift you need as you eagerly wait for the return of our Lord Jesus Christ.

1 CORINTHIANS 1:7

The godly will flourish like palm trees and grow strong like the cedars of Lebanon. For they are transplanted to the LORD's own house. They flourish in the courts of our God. Even in old age they will still produce fruit; they will remain vital and green.

PSALM 92:12-14

True godliness with contentment is itself great wealth. After all, we brought nothing with us when we came into the world, and we can't take anything with us when we leave it. So if we have enough food and clothing, let us be content.

1 TIMOTHY 6:6-8

Give generously to the poor, not grudgingly, for the LORD your God will bless you in everything you do.

DEUTERONOMY 15:10

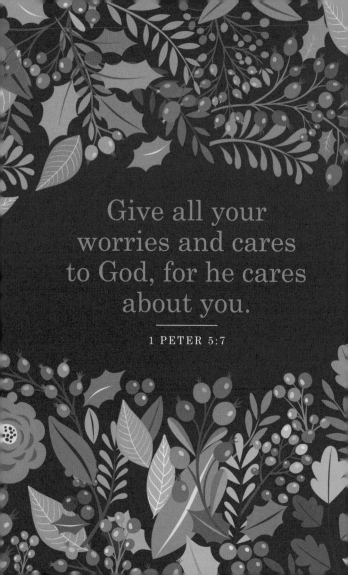

Give all your
worries and cares
to God, for he cares
about you.

———

1 PETER 5:7

Every time I think of you, I give thanks to my God. Whenever I pray, I make my requests for all of you with joy. . . . And I am certain that God, who began the good work within you, will continue his work until it is finally finished on the day when Christ Jesus returns.

PHILIPPIANS 1:3-4, 6

God is the one who provides seed for
the farmer and then bread to eat. In the
same way, he will provide and increase
your resources and then produce a great
harvest of generosity in you. Yes, you will
be enriched in every way so that you can
always be generous. And when we take your
gifts to those who need them, they will
thank God.

2 CORINTHIANS 9:10-11

Let your good
deeds shine out
for all to see, so that
everyone will praise your
heavenly Father.

MATTHEW 5:16

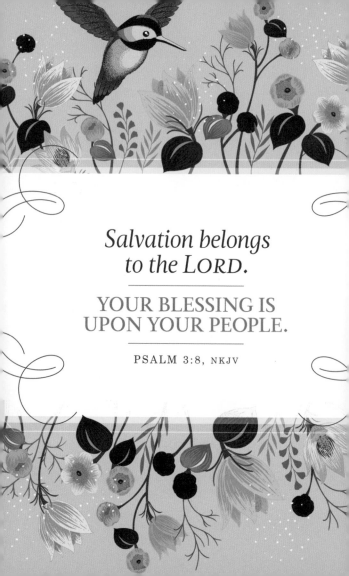

*Salvation belongs
to the LORD.*

YOUR BLESSING IS
UPON YOUR PEOPLE.

PSALM 3:8, NKJV

Since we have been made right in God's sight
by the blood of Christ, he will certainly
save us from God's condemnation. For since
our friendship with God was restored by
the death of his Son while we were still his
enemies, we will certainly be saved through
the life of his Son.

ROMANS 5:9-10

I love you, LORD; you are my strength. . . .
I called on the LORD, who is worthy of
praise, and he saved me from my enemies.
. . . He reached down from heaven and
rescued me. . . . He led me to a place of
safety; he rescued me because he delights
in me.

PSALM 18:1, 3, 16, 19

He has showered
his kindness on us,
along with
all wisdom and
understanding.

EPHESIANS 1:8

God blesses those who work for peace, for they will be called children of God.

MATTHEW 5:9

I know the LORD is always with me. I will
not be shaken, for he is right beside me. No
wonder my heart is glad, and I rejoice. My
body rests in safety. For you will not leave
my soul among the dead. . . . You will show
me the way of life, granting me the joy of
your presence and the pleasures of living
with you forever.

PSALM 16:8-11

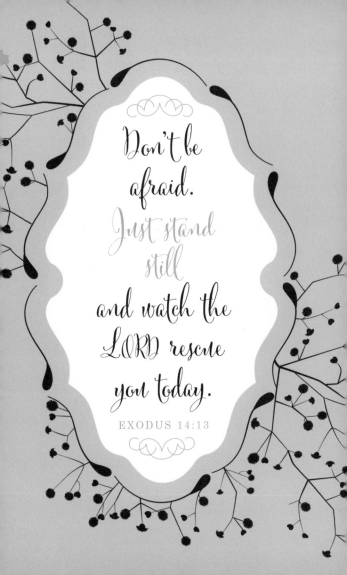

Don't be afraid. Just stand still and watch the LORD rescue you today.

EXODUS 14:13

How sweet your
words taste to me;
they are sweeter
than honey.

PSALM 119:103

We were therefore buried with him through baptism into death in order that, just as Christ was raised from the dead through the glory of the Father, we too may live a new life. For if we have been united with him in a death like his, we will certainly also be united with him in a resurrection like his.

ROMANS 6:4-5, NIV

Righteousness and justice are the foundation of your throne; love and faithfulness go before you. Blessed are those who have learned to acclaim you, who walk in the light of your presence, LORD. They rejoice in your name all day long; they celebrate your righteousness. For you are their glory and strength.

PSALM 89:14-17, NIV

God blesses those who hunger and thirst for justice, for they will be satisfied.

MATTHEW 5:6

We can rejoice in our wonderful new relationship with God because our Lord Jesus Christ has made us friends of God.

ROMANS 5:11

The LORD is compassionate and merciful, slow
to get angry and filled with unfailing love.
He will not constantly accuse us, nor remain
angry forever. He does not punish us for all
our sins; he does not deal harshly with us,
as we deserve. For his unfailing love toward
those who fear him is as great as the
height of the heavens above the earth.

PSALM 103:8-11

Since God chose you to be the holy people he loves, you must clothe yourselves with tenderhearted mercy, kindness, humility, gentleness, and patience. Make allowance for each other's faults, and forgive anyone who offends you. Remember, the Lord forgave you, so you must forgive others.

COLOSSIANS 3:12-13

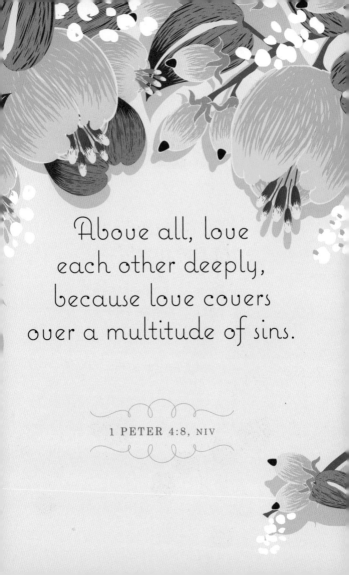

Above all, love
each other deeply,
because love covers
over a multitude of sins.

1 PETER 4:8, NIV

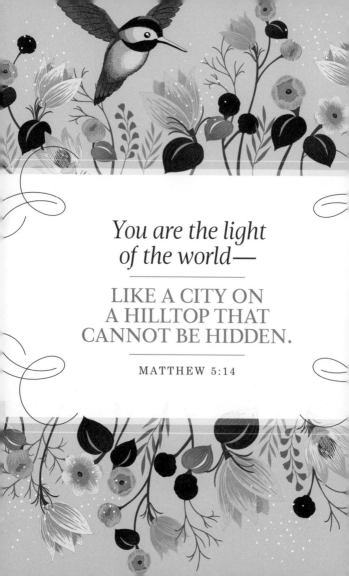

You are the light of the world—

LIKE A CITY ON
A HILLTOP THAT
CANNOT BE HIDDEN.

MATTHEW 5:14

The LORD lives! Praise to my Rock! May the God of my salvation be exalted! He is the God who . . . rescues me from my enemies. You hold me safe beyond the reach of my enemies; you save me from violent opponents. For this, O LORD, I will praise you among the nations; I will sing praises to your name.

PSALM 18:46-49

When you came down long ago, you
did awesome deeds beyond our highest
expectations. And oh, how the mountains
quaked! For since the world began, no ear
has heard and no eye has seen a God
like you, who works for those who wait
for him! You welcome those who gladly
do good, who follow godly ways.

ISAIAH 64:3-5

The LORD
watches over
the path of
the godly.

PSALM 1:6

Blessed are those who honor my Sabbath days of rest and keep themselves from doing wrong.

ISAIAH 56:2

Blessed be your glorious name, and may it
be exalted above all blessing and praise.
You alone are the LORD. You made the
heavens, even the highest heavens, and all
their starry host, the earth and all that is
on it, the seas and all that is in them. You
give life to everything, and the multitudes
of heaven worship you.

NEHEMIAH 9:5-6, NIV

You are our
Father. We are
the clay, and

you are
the potter.
We all are formed
by your hand.

ISAIAH 64:8

These things
I have spoken
to you, that
My joy may
remain in you,
and that your
joy may be full.

JOHN 15:11, NKJV

Let us lay aside every weight, and the sin which so easily ensnares us, and let us run with endurance the race that is set before us, looking unto Jesus, the author and finisher of our faith, who for the joy that was set before Him endured the cross, despising the shame, and has sat down at the right hand of the throne of God.

HEBREWS 12:1-2, NKJV

You are a letter from Christ delivered by us, written not with ink but with the Spirit of the living God, not on tablets of stone but on tablets of human hearts. Such is the confidence that we have through Christ toward God. Not that we are sufficient in ourselves to claim anything as coming from us, but our sufficiency is from God.

2 CORINTHIANS 3:3-5, ESV

*Those who live
in accordance
with the Spirit*
*have their
minds set on
what the
Spirit desires.*

ROMANS 8:5, NIV

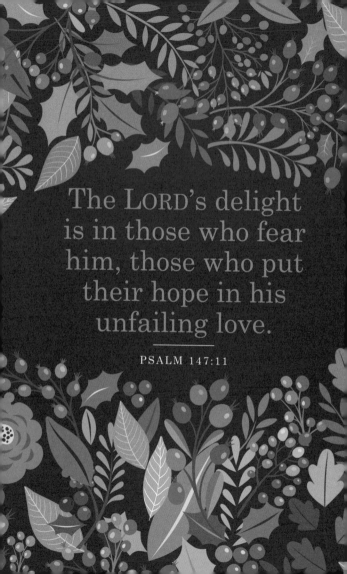

The LORD's delight
is in those who fear
him, those who put
their hope in his
unfailing love.

PSALM 147:11

You are my hiding place; you protect me from trouble. You surround me with songs of victory. . . . Many sorrows come to the wicked, but unfailing love surrounds those who trust the LORD. So rejoice in the LORD and be glad, all you who obey him! Shout for joy, all you whose hearts are pure!

PSALM 32:7, 10-11

Dear friends, we are already God's children, but he has not yet shown us what we will be like when Christ appears. But we do know that we will be like him, for we will see him as he really is. And all who have this eager expectation will keep themselves pure, just as he is pure.

1 JOHN 3:2-3

God blesses
those whose hearts
are pure, for they
will see God.

MATTHEW 5:8

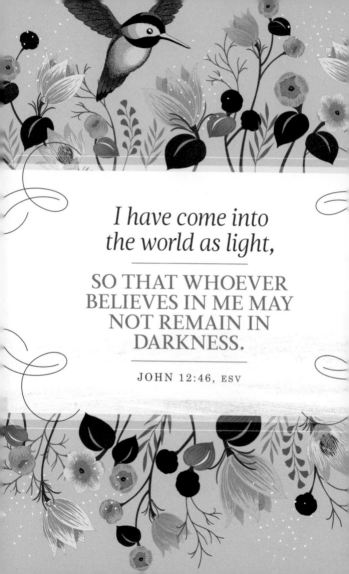

I have come into the world as light,

SO THAT WHOEVER BELIEVES IN ME MAY NOT REMAIN IN DARKNESS.

JOHN 12:46, ESV

"I will answer," says the LORD. "I will answer the sky as it pleads for clouds. And the sky will answer the earth with rain. Then the earth will answer the thirsty cries of the grain, the grapevines, and the olive trees. . . . I will show love to those I called 'Not loved.' And to those I called 'Not my people,' I will say, 'Now you are my people.'"

HOSEA 2:21-23

How priceless is your unfailing love, O God!
People take refuge in the shadow of your
wings. They feast on the abundance of your
house; you give them drink from your river
of delights. For with you is the fountain
of life; in your light we see light. Continue
your love to those who know you, your
righteousness to the upright in heart.

PSALM 36:7-10, NIV

Take delight in
the LORD, and

he will give you

*your heart's
desires.*

PSALM 37:4

In the world
you will have
tribulation.
But take heart:
I have overcome
the world.

JOHN 16:33, ESV

Loving God means keeping his commandments, and his commandments are not burdensome. For every child of God defeats this evil world, and we achieve this victory through our faith. And who can win this battle against the world? Only those who believe that Jesus is the Son of God.

1 JOHN 5:3-5

I can do all things
through Christ
who strengthens me.

PHILIPPIANS 4:13, NKJV

The LORD...
blesses the home
of the upright.

PROVERBS 3:33

Children, obey your parents because you belong to the Lord, for this is the right thing to do. "Honor your father and mother." This is the first commandment with a promise: If you honor your father and mother, "things will go well for you, and you will have a long life on the earth."

EPHESIANS 6:1-3

I tell you, keep on asking, and you will receive what you ask for. Keep on seeking, and you will find. Keep on knocking, and the door will be opened to you. For everyone who asks, receives. Everyone who seeks, finds. And to everyone who knocks, the door will be opened.

LUKE 11:9-10

Because I am
righteous,
I will see you.
When I awake,
I will see
you face to
face and be
satisfied.

PSALM 17:15

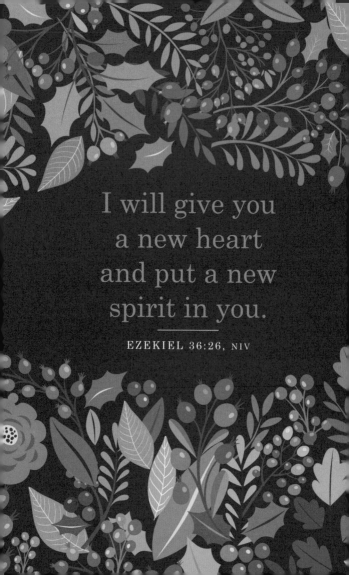

I will give you
a new heart
and put a new
spirit in you.

EZEKIEL 36:26, NIV

Now the Lord is the Spirit, and where the
Spirit of the Lord is, there is freedom. And
we all, with unveiled face, beholding the
glory of the Lord, are being transformed
into the same image from one degree of
glory to another. For this comes from the
Lord who is the Spirit.

2 CORINTHIANS 3:17-18, ESV

Give, and you will receive. Your gift will return to you in full—pressed down, shaken together to make room for more, running over, and poured into your lap. The amount you give will determine the amount you get back.

LUKE 6:38

Whatever is
good and perfect
is a gift coming
down to us from
God our Father.

JAMES 1:17

*All glory to God,
who . . . will bring you
with great joy into his
glorious presence*

WITHOUT A
SINGLE FAULT.

JUDE 1:24

He will keep you strong to the end so
that you will be free from all blame on the
day when our Lord Jesus Christ returns.
God will do this, for he is faithful to do
what he says, and he has invited you into
partnership with his Son, Jesus Christ
our Lord.

1 CORINTHIANS 1:8-9

When the Father sends the Advocate as my
representative—that is, the Holy Spirit—he
will teach you everything and will remind
you of everything I have told you. I am
leaving you with a gift—peace of mind and
heart. And the peace I give is a gift the
world cannot give. So don't be troubled
or afraid.

JOHN 14:26-27

Peacemakers who
sow in peace reap
a harvest of
righteousness.

JAMES 3:18, NIV

God blesses those who are poor and realize their need for him, for the Kingdom of Heaven is theirs.

MATTHEW 5:3

Whoever looks intently into the perfect law that gives freedom, and continues in it—not forgetting what they have heard, but doing it—they will be blessed in what they do. . . . Religion that God our Father accepts as pure and faultless is this: to look after orphans and widows in their distress and to keep oneself from being polluted by the world.

JAMES 1:25, 27, NIV

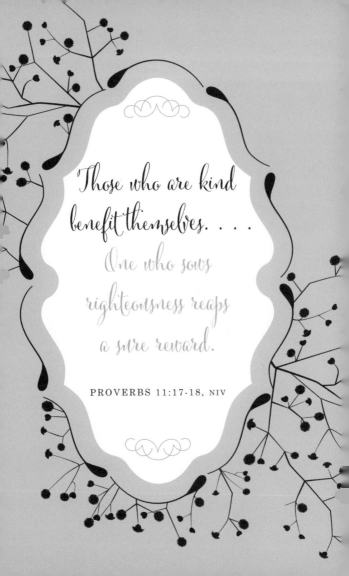

Those who are kind
benefit themselves. . . .
One who sows
righteousness reaps
a sure reward.

PROVERBS 11:17-18, NIV

As a father
shows compassion
to his children,
so the LORD
shows compassion to
those who fear him.

PSALM 103:13, ESV

Sing for joy, O heavens! Rejoice, O earth!
. . . For the LORD has comforted his people
and will have compassion on them in their
suffering. . . . Can a mother forget her
nursing child? Can she feel no love for
the child she has borne? But even if that
were possible, I would not forget you! See,
I have written your name on the palms of
my hands.

ISAIAH 49:13, 15-16

The LORD is a great God. . . . He holds in his hands the depths of the earth and the mightiest mountains. The sea belongs to him, for he made it. His hands formed the dry land, too. Come, let us worship and bow down. Let us kneel before the LORD our maker, for he is our God. We are the people he watches over, the flock under his care.

PSALM 95:3-7

You are my
refuge and
my shield;
your word
is my source
of hope.

PSALM 119:114

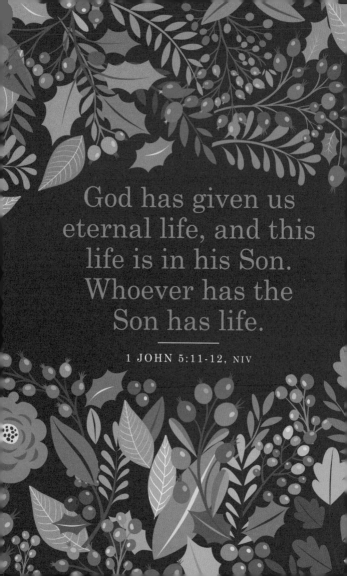

God has given us
eternal life, and this
life is in his Son.
Whoever has the
Son has life.

1 JOHN 5:11-12, NIV

Learn to do good. Seek justice. Help the oppressed. Defend the cause of orphans. Fight for the rights of widows. "Come now, let's settle this," says the LORD. "Though your sins are like scarlet, I will make them as white as snow. Though they are red like crimson, I will make them as white as wool."

ISAIAH 1:17-18

The Lord himself will come down from heaven with a commanding shout. . . . First, the believers who have died will rise from their graves. Then, together with them, we who are still alive and remain on the earth will be caught up in the clouds to meet the Lord in the air. Then we will be with the Lord forever. So encourage each other with these words.

1 THESSALONIANS 4:16-18

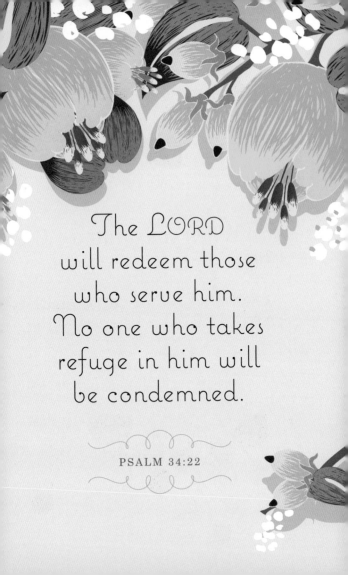

The LORD
will redeem those
who serve him.
No one who takes
refuge in him will
be condemned.

PSALM 34:22

When you grant a
blessing to your servant,

O SOVEREIGN Lord, IT IS
AN ETERNAL BLESSING!

2 SAMUEL 7:29

"I know the plans I have for you," declares the LORD, "plans to prosper you and not to harm you, plans to give you hope and a future. Then you will call on me and come and pray to me, and I will listen to you."

JEREMIAH 29:11-12, NIV

Whoever wants to be a leader among you must be your servant, and whoever wants to be first among you must become your slave. For even the Son of Man came not to be served but to serve others and to give his life as a ransom for many.

MATTHEW 20:26-28

Be devoted to one
another in love.
Honor one
another above
yourselves.

ROMANS 12:10, NIV

If it is possible, as far as it depends on you, live at peace with everyone.

ROMANS 12:18, NIV

When my life was ebbing away, I remembered you, LORD, and my prayer rose to you, to your holy temple. . . . I, with shouts of grateful praise, will sacrifice to you. What I have vowed I will make good. I will say, "Salvation comes from the LORD."

JONAH 2:7, 9, NIV

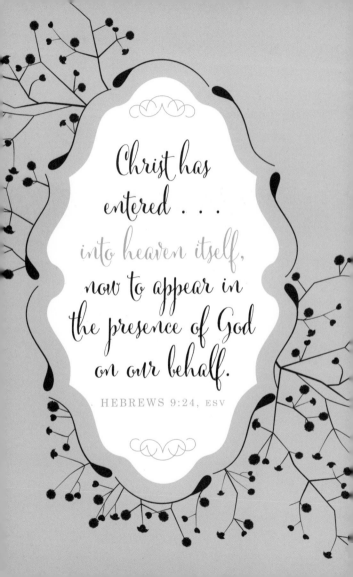

Christ has
entered . . .
into heaven itself,
now to appear in
the presence of God
on our behalf.

HEBREWS 9:24, ESV

Draw near to
God, and
he will draw
near to you.

JAMES 4:8, ESV

Jesus called a little child to him and put the child among them. Then he said, "I tell you the truth, unless you turn from your sins and become like little children, you will never get into the Kingdom of Heaven. So anyone who becomes as humble as this little child is the greatest in the Kingdom of Heaven."

MATTHEW 18:2-4

God has given each of you a gift from his great variety of spiritual gifts. Use them well to serve one another. . . . Then everything you do will bring glory to God through Jesus Christ. All glory and power to him forever and ever! Amen.

1 PETER 4:10-11

Whoever sows
sparingly
will also reap
sparingly, and
whoever sows
bountifully
will also reap
bountifully.

2 CORINTHIANS 9:6, ESV

The Spirit himself
testifies with our
spirit that we are
God's children.

ROMANS 8:16, NIV

All praise to God, the Father of our Lord
Jesus Christ, who has blessed us with every
spiritual blessing in the heavenly realms
because we are united with Christ. Even
before he made the world, God loved us and
chose us in Christ to be holy and without
fault in his eyes.

EPHESIANS 1:3-4

Learn to know the God of your ancestors intimately. Worship and serve him with your whole heart and a willing mind. For the LORD sees every heart and knows every plan and thought. If you seek him, you will find him.

1 CHRONICLES 28:9

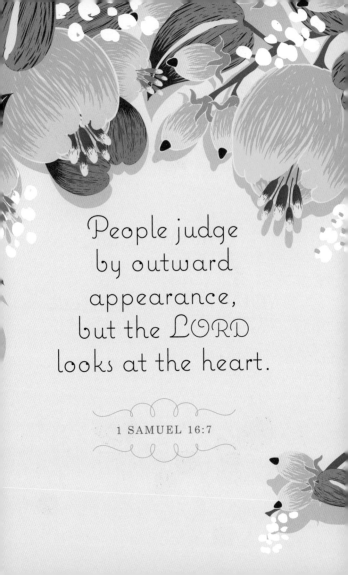

People judge
by outward
appearance,
but the LORD
looks at the heart.

1 SAMUEL 16:7

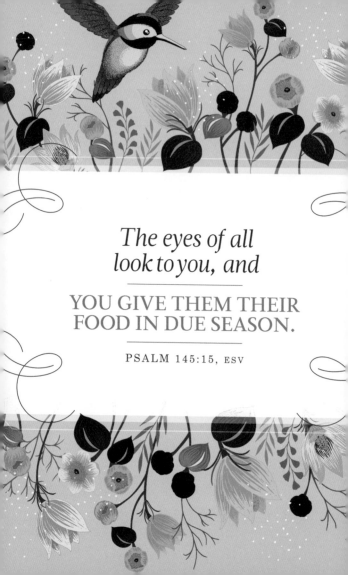

The eyes of all
look to you, and

YOU GIVE THEM THEIR
FOOD IN DUE SEASON.

PSALM 145:15, ESV

Why do you worry about clothing? Consider the lilies of the field, how they grow: they neither toil nor spin; and yet I say to you that even Solomon in all his glory was not arrayed like one of these. Now if God so clothes the grass of the field, which today is, and tomorrow is thrown into the oven, will He not much more clothe you?

MATTHEW 6:28-30, NKJV

The time is coming—indeed it's here now—
when true worshipers will worship the
Father in spirit and in truth. The Father is
looking for those who will worship him that
way. For God is Spirit, so those who worship
him must worship in spirit and in truth.

JOHN 4:23-24

Jesus and the
ones he makes holy

have the
same Father.

HEBREWS 2:11

O LORD,
what a variety
of things you
have made!
In wisdom
you have made
them all.

PSALM 104:24

I said, "You are my servant"; I have chosen
you and have not rejected you. So do not
fear, for I am with you; do not be dismayed,
for I am your God. I will strengthen you
and help you; I will uphold you with my
righteous right hand.

ISAIAH 41:9-10, NIV

The LORD is
righteous
in everything he
does; he is filled
with kindness.

PSALM 145:17

You have heard my vows, O God. You have given me an inheritance reserved for those who fear your name.

PSALM 61:5

How great is the goodness you have stored up for those who fear you. You lavish it on those who come to you for protection, blessing them before the watching world. . . . Praise the LORD, for he has shown me the wonders of his unfailing love. . . . So be strong and courageous, all you who put your hope in the LORD!

PSALM 31:19, 21, 24

Don't copy the behavior and customs of this world, but let God transform you into a new person by changing the way you think. Then you will learn to know God's will for you, which is good and pleasing and perfect.

ROMANS 12:2

*If we confess
our sins
to him,*
*he is faithful
and just to
forgive us.*

1 JOHN 1:9

Share each other's burdens, and in this way obey the law of Christ.

GALATIANS 6:2

Let us not become weary in doing good, for at the proper time we will reap a harvest if we do not give up. Therefore, as we have opportunity, let us do good to all people, especially to those who belong to the family of believers.

GALATIANS 6:9-10, NIV

This is how God loved the world: He gave his one and only Son, so that everyone who believes in him will not perish but have eternal life. God sent his Son into the world not to judge the world, but to save the world through him.

JOHN 3:16-17

When everything
is ready, I will come
and get you, so that
you will always be
with me where I am.

JOHN 14:3

God blesses those who are persecuted for doing right,

FOR THE KINGDOM OF HEAVEN IS THEIRS.

MATTHEW 5:10

Blessed is the man who remains steadfast under trial, for when he has stood the test he will receive the crown of life, which God has promised to those who love him. . . . Therefore put away all filthiness and rampant wickedness and receive with meekness the implanted word, which is able to save your souls.

JAMES 1:12, 21, ESV

You hold my right hand. You guide me with
your counsel, leading me to a glorious
destiny. Whom have I in heaven but you?
I desire you more than anything on earth.
My health may fail, and my spirit may grow
weak, but God remains the strength of my
heart; he is mine forever.

PSALM 73:23-26

I will praise the LORD, who counsels me; even at night my heart instructs me.

Come, you who are blessed by my Father, inherit the Kingdom prepared for you from the creation of the world.

MATTHEW 25:34

Study this Book of Instruction continually. Meditate on it day and night so you will be sure to obey everything written in it. Only then will you prosper and succeed in all you do. This is my command—be strong and courageous! Do not be afraid or discouraged. For the LORD your God is with you wherever you go.

JOSHUA 1:8-9

Praise the LORD.
Blessed are those
who fear the LORD,
who find great delight
in his commands.

PSALM 112:1, NIV

*God blesses those
who are merciful,
for they will be
shown mercy.*

MATTHEW 5:7

It was our weaknesses he carried; it was our sorrows that weighed him down. And we thought his troubles were a punishment from God, a punishment for his own sins! But he was pierced for our rebellion, crushed for our sins. He was beaten so we could be whole. He was whipped so we could be healed.

ISAIAH 53:4-5

When we were utterly helpless, Christ came at just the right time and died for us sinners. Now, most people would not be willing to die for an upright person, though someone might perhaps be willing to die for a person who is especially good. But God showed his great love for us by sending Christ to die for us while we were still sinners.

ROMANS 5:6-8

Jesus answered,
"I am the
way and the
truth and
the life."

JOHN 14:6, NIV

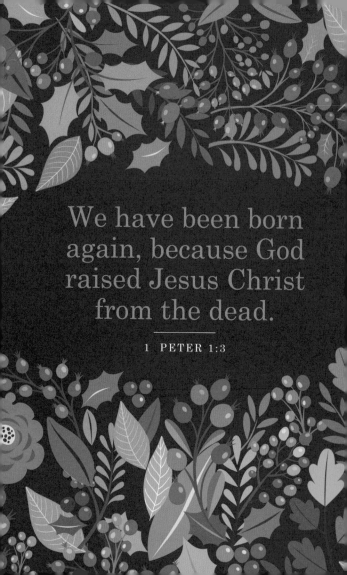

We have been born
again, because God
raised Jesus Christ
from the dead.

1 PETER 1:3

I saw a Lamb that looked as if it had been slaughtered, but it was now standing between the throne and the four living beings and among the twenty-four elders. . . . And they sang a new song with these words: "You are worthy. . . . For you were slaughtered, and your blood has ransomed people for God from every tribe and language and people and nation. And you have caused them to become a Kingdom of priests for our God. And they will reign on the earth."

REVELATION 5:6, 9-10

I heard the voices of thousands and millions of angels around the throne and of the living beings and the elders. And they sang in a mighty chorus: "Worthy is the Lamb who was slaughtered—to receive power and riches and wisdom and strength and honor and glory and blessing."

REVELATION 5:11-12

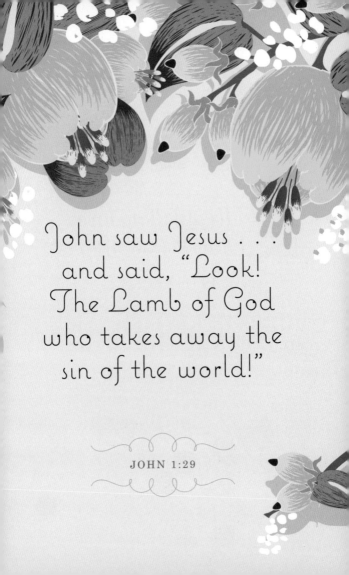

John saw Jesus . . .
and said, "Look!
The Lamb of God
who takes away the
sin of the world!"

JOHN 1:29

*His unfailing love
for us is powerful;*

THE LORD'S
FAITHFULNESS
ENDURES FOREVER.
PRAISE THE LORD!

PSALM 117:2

Look, God's home is now among his people!
He will live with them, and they will be his
people. God himself will be with them. He will
wipe every tear from their eyes, and there
will be no more death or sorrow or crying or
pain. All these things are gone forever.

REVELATION 21:3-4

LIVING EXPRESSIONS
COLLECTION

Living Expressions invites you to explore God's Word and express your creativity in ways that are refreshing to the spirit and restorative to the soul.

Visit Tyndale online at www.tyndale.com.

TYNDALE, Tyndale's quill logo, *Living Expressions*, and the Living Expressions logo are registered trademarks of Tyndale House Publishers, Inc.

A Bouquet of Beautiful Blessings to Warm Your Heart

Compilation copyright © 2018 by Tyndale House Publishers, Inc. All rights reserved.

Cover illustration of curly border copyright © Drew Melton/Creative Market; all rights reserved. Cover illustration of floral elements copyright © The Autumn Rabbit Ltd/Creative Market; all rights reserved. Cover photograph of watercolor texture copyright © ArtistMef/Creative Market; all rights reserved.

Interior illustrations are from Adobe Stock and are the properties of their respective copyright holders, and all rights are reserved. Floral frame copyright © Miroslava Hlavacoca; watercolor flower copyright © Julia Dreams; vibrant flowers copyright © Oksancia; floral backgrounds copyright © moleskostudio; floral border and bird copyright © Sukhyun; floral graphic copyright © kollibri.

Cover design by Cathryn Pratt. Interior design by Nicole Grimes.

Unless otherwise indicated, all Scripture quotations are taken from the *Holy Bible*, New Living Translation, copyright © 1996, 2004, 2007, 2013, 2015 by Tyndale House Foundation; used by permission of Tyndale House Publishers, Inc., Carol Stream, Illinois 60188; all rights reserved. Scripture quotations marked ESV are taken from *The Holy Bible*, English Standard Version® (ESV®), copyright © 2001 by Crossway, a publishing ministry of Good News Publishers; used by permission; all rights reserved. Scripture quotations marked NIV are taken from the Holy Bible, *New International Version*,® NIV,® copyright © 1973, 1978, 1984, 2011 by Biblica, Inc.®; used by permission; all rights reserved worldwide. Scripture quotations marked NKJV are taken from the New King James Version,® copyright © 1982 by Thomas Nelson, Inc.; used by permission; all rights reserved. Scripture quotations marked TLB are taken from *The Living Bible*, copyright © 1971 by Tyndale House Foundation; used by permission of Tyndale House Publishers, Inc., Carol Stream, Illinois 60188; all rights reserved.

For information about special discounts for bulk purchases, please contact Tyndale House Publishers at csresponse@tyndale.com, or call 1-800-323-9400.

ISBN 978-1-4964-3607-8

Printed in China

24   23   22   21   20   19   18
7   6   5   4   3   2   1